Wishing you the best for this holiday winters and a much better new year – we believe in you, there is hope, we have resources to explore, and you are loved – big hugs,

Deb : Connt

The **HEDGEHOG** got its peculiar
name in part because of its
pig-like snout and the grunts it
makes as it roots through the
undergrowth for food.

The bristles along a **VENUS FLYTRAP'S** jaws work like prison bars, keeping jittery insects from making their escape.

MANY SPECIES OF BLOWFISH CONTAIN A TOXIN
1,200 TIMES MORE DEADLY THAN CYANIDE.
IN SPITE OF THE DANGER, THIS FISH IS STILL
CONSIDERED A DELICACY IN SOME COUNTRIES.

The **PRICKLY PEAR'S** broad green pads,
which soak up the desert sun, are actually
its branches. Its leaves are the splintery spines
that grow along the surface of the pads.

Baby **ECHIDNAS**, called "puggles," hatch from a soft, leathery shell. Like the platypus, the echidna is one of the few mammals to lay eggs.

THE MOST POPULAR ALOE PLANT, ALOE VERA, IS USED AS A TOPICAL REMEDY FOR SUNBURN AND DRY SKIN. IT'S FOUND IN EVERYTHING FROM BEAUTY PRODUCTS TO BOTTLED DRINKS.

The grooves on the
THORNY DEVIL'S scaly
skin help direct drops
of water toward its
mouth—the lizard then
laps the liquid up with
its sticky tongue.

Over its lifetime, a **SEA URCHIN**
shows few signs of aging.
The oldest known specimen was
found to be about 200 years old!

BECAUSE THESE CLUMSY CRITTERS WILL OFTEN STICK THEMSELVES
BY ACCIDENT, EACH PORCUPINE QUILL IS COATED IN A
NATURAL ANTIBIOTIC TO PREVENT AGAINST SELF-HARM.

The **SAGUARO'S** pleated outer surface allows it to expand as it takes on water.

WHEN HEDGEHOGS ENCOUNTER A NEW OR UNUSUAL
SMELL, THEY REACT BY LICKING FOAMY SALIVA
ONTO THEIR SPINES. THIS ODDBALL BEHAVIOR
IS CALLED "SELF-ANOINTING."

Tiny hairs detect motion on the surface of the **VENUS FLYTRAP'S** petals. If the plant senses at least two movements in twenty seconds, it abruptly clamps shut.

When provoked, a **BLOWFISH** will puff itself up to three times its original size, sending sharp spines radiating outward.

THE PRICKLY PEAR FRUIT IS
ALSO KNOWN AS "TUNA."

ECHIDNAS are *slow*. In fact, their slow metabolism is credited with helping them live up to 50 years.

ALOE is a type of succulent, a fleshy plant that possesses a juicy pulp. The word "succulent" comes from the Latin for "juice."

THE SCALY KNOB ON THE BACK OF THIS REPTILE
IS KNOWN AS A "FALSE HEAD." WHEN THREATENED,
A THORNY DEVIL WILL TUCK DOWN ITS REAL HEAD
AND LEAVE THIS CLEVER DECOY EXPOSED.

A **SEA URCHIN'S** body is an example
of five-fold, radial symmetry,
meaning it can be sliced into five
identical portions like a birthday cake.

"PORCUPINE" comes from a combination of the Latin words for "pig" and "spine."

ON AVERAGE, A SAGUARO HOLDS
ABOUT A FULL TON OF WATER INSIDE
ITS STEMS. AT PEAK HYDRATION,
IT WEIGHS ROUGHLY 4,000 POUNDS.

HEDGEHOGS are nocturnal, sleeping up to eighteen hours a day and foraging in the nighttime.

DESPITE ITS DIETARY QUIRKS,
A VENUS FLYTRAP IS JUST LIKE
ANY OTHER PLANT. IT NEEDS
A NORMAL INTAKE OF SUNLIGHT,
GASES, AND WATER TO SURVIVE.

When outside the water a
BLOWFISH is able to fill itself
up with air instead of liquid.

The flesh of this cactus has been shown to purify water, inspiring scientists to explore how the **PRICKLY PEAR** might be used as a low-cost method of water treatment.

THE ECHIDNA HAS A SPECIAL
SUPER POWER: THE ABILITY
TO PICK UP ELECTRICAL SIGNALS
WITH ITS SNOUT.

Ancient Greeks and Romans used
ALOE VERA to treat wounds.
The translucent gel in its leaves
possesses special microbe-fighting
compounds called saponins.

The **THORNY DEVIL** changes color with the temperature. It begins the cool desert morning a dark greenish brown and turns a pale yellow as the sun rises.

SEA URCHINS POSSESS
A CREEPY-LOOKING MOUTH
CALLED "ARISTOTLE'S LANTERN,"
IDEAL FOR SCRAPING ALGAE
OFF THE OCEAN FLOOR.

Besides its most obvious
defense mechanism,
a **PORCUPINE** will loudly
clack its teeth together
as a way of saying
"back off!"

THE SAGUARO CAN GROW TO OVER
40 FEET TALL. THE TALLEST KNOWN
SAGUARO WAS MEASURED AT SIX
AND A HALF STORIES TALL!

A group of **HEDGEHOGS** is called a "prickle," though it's rare to see one because this species prefers to spend most of its time alone.

Once shut, the **FLYTRAP** secretes
digestive juices that work on its prey for
a week or so. Then the petals open up
again, ready for the next meal.

DRIED—OUT BLOWFISH ARE OFTEN USED FOR DECORATIVE
PURPOSES. THEY'VE BEEN TURNED INTO WHIMSICAL
LANTERNS AND WAR HELMETS ALIKE.

The cochineal—an insect that lives on the **PRICKLY PEAR** cactus—is known for containing a brilliant red acid used in various dyes and food coloring.

The long-beaked **ECHIDNA** even has tiny spines along its tongue, which it uses to collect insect prey.

ALOE VERA'S BITTER TASTE
AND SPIKY LEAVES HELP
PROTECT IT FROM PREDATORS.

The **THORNY DEVIL** has a funny walk, which involves frequent stopping and wiggling. This is thought to conceal its appearance from predators.

To move around, a **SEA URCHIN** will either use its spines or a special arrangement of sucker-tipped feet on its underside.

A PORCUPINE'S QUILLS START OUT SOFT AT BIRTH
AND HARDEN WITHIN A FEW SHORT DAYS.